The Christ-Life
for
The Self-Life

The Christ-Life

FOR

The Self-Life

(Formerly "A CASTAWAY")

by

F. B. MEYER

CHICAGO
MOODY PRESS

These Addresses were delivered at the Carnegie Hall, New York, during an ever-memorable week, and in part also, at the Tremont Temple Boston, and in Philadelphia. In answer to many urgent demands they are printed almost as they were delivered, from the reporter's notes: therefore may lack in literary finish—but the truth is the main consideration. And I believe that what is taught here will give a glimpse into those deeper aspects of Christianity, which are best adapted to nourish and quicken the inner life.

F. B. Meyer

TABLE OF CONTENTS

A CASTAWAY

I INVITE YOUR ATTENTION to a few words found in I Corinthians 9:27: "Lest that by any means, when I have preached to others, I myself should be a castaway."

Paul was too eager and too practical a man to dally with a bogey dread. Since then he intimates that it was his daily fear lest, after having preached to others, he might himself be a castaway, I suppose that there were but few hours in his life when this dread did not haunt him. After he had founded so many churches, written so many epistles, and exercised so widespread an influence, in his quiet moments he was perpetually face to face with this awful nightmare, that the day might come when he would be a castaway; and the thought drove him almost to madness. When he was traveling over the blue Ægean, when he was sitting making his tents, when he was engaged in dictating his epistles, the thought would come back and back upon his heart, "I may yet be a castaway."

Have you ever feared this? I am not sure that a man ever reaches his highest development without something of the element of fear, and I ask you now if in your life you know something of this haunting dread. May I confess to you that it has become a great dread of my own? and if many days pass, and no one writes to tell me of help derived from my ministry, and no one comes to join our church, and no one seems to be influenced by my life or word, I sit myself down and say, "Good God, has the time come at last to me when for some reason I, too, am to be a castaway?"

And reverently, humbly, but most searchingly, I ask you, my reader, whether it may not be possible that this very moment you are already a castaway.

"A CASTAWAY" IN WHAT SENSE?

Is it to be supposed for a moment that the Apostle thought that when once the believer has fled to Christ he can be cast out into the outer darkness where there is weeping, and wailing, and gnashing of teeth? Is it possible for a limb to be torn from the mystical body of Christ, for a jewel to be snatched from out of His crown, for a sheep to be devoured from His flock? Are there any unfinished pictures in God's gallery, any incomplete statues in His workshop? Does God begin a work in the soul and leave it incomplete and unperfected? We cannot believe it.

It is said of Rowland Hill, my great predecessor at Christ Church, London, that when an old man of eighty-four and just before he died, one Sunday night when the lights had been put out in Surrey Chapel, the verger in attendance heard him go to and fro in the aisle, singing to himself:

> When I am to die, "Receive me"—I'll cry,
> For Jesus has loved me, I cannot tell why;
> But this I do find, we two are so joined,
> He'll not be in heaven and leave me behind.

If you have faith as a grain of mustard seed, if it is directed toward Christ, a union has been formed between

Him and you which neither heaven nor earth nor hell nor time nor eternity can ever break.

And yet the Apostle feared he would be a castaway. What did he mean?

One day I was calling on a brother clergyman. He took me out into his garden to an outhouse, against the side of which was resting one of the old-fashioned bicycles with a very tall wheel. I said to him, "Do you ever ride this?"

Said he, "No; see how rusty it is. I have not been on it for many months. I have got something better, something that suits my purpose better," pointing to another and a newer bicycle on the other side of the house.

I said to myself, "Then this is a castaway."

When stylographic pens first came out, I purchased one in the hope that it would serve me perfectly. But I was sadly disappointed. Sometimes when I attempted to use it, it was unwilling to serve me. At other times it was profuse in inking the finger. Finally I discarded it in hopelessness and purchased another pen. The one I now hold serves me perfectly, and I have no difficulty whatever in performing by its means any writing upon which I have set my heart. But I keep the other one. It lies in the drawer of my bureau, and often when I am putting my things together to go upon some journey, I think I hear it saying to itself as it lies there, "Ah, he is going away without me again! There was a time when he never left home without taking me with him; he never wrote a letter without me; he never composed an article but that I first knew its contents; but for these many days and months I have been lying here unused."

That disused stylographic pen is my conception of what Paul meant when he said he feared being a castaway.

You must know that this man loved to save men. It was the passion of his life. Send him to Philippi, and he will not be there a day before he has turned the devil out of the poor demoniac girl. Let him be put in jail, and before midnight he will have baptized his jailer. Send him to Athens, and though he is all alone, he will gather a congregation upon Mars' Hill within a week or two. Put him alongside of Aquila and Priscilla at the bench, and he will make tents and talk to them in such good wise that they will become Christians. Stand him before his judge, and the latter will cry, "Almost thou persuadest me to be a Christian!" Let him go to Rome, tied to a Roman sentry, and he will speak to these men, one after another, in such fashion that the whole Pretorian camp will be infused with the love of God. His passion was to save men. I do not believe that if he were alive to-day, he would be in a streetcar, or a railway car, or on board a steamer without buttonholing some man and speaking to him about his soul and his Saviour. The whole passion of the man was to save some; but he feared that unless he took good care, the hour might come in his life when Christ would say, "Thou hast served me well, but thou shalt serve me no more. Of late thou hast become indolent, and choked with pride, and I have not secured thy whole obedience. I am now compelled to call upon some soul more alert, more obedient than thee; and that man I will use to do the work that thou mightest have done, but which thou didst fail to accomplish."

This comes home upon us, brother ministers. I am speaking to some who in their earlier life were wondrously used of God in soul-winning, as they went from the seminary or the college, and took their first church.

Sunday after Sunday the inquiry-room was crowded. The simple villagers, from their lips, heard the Word of God, and were converted, and the communicant's roll was weekly increased. The boys of the neighborhood were attracted, and won like jewels for Christ. Am I not speaking to women who in their first burst of love to Christ wore the signs of holy earnestness in their circles of society, so that all who came in contact with them were made to feel the power of a genuine love to God? May we not all look back to days upon days, long passed, when we were the channels through which Jesus spoke and wrought, and the Holy Ghost was poured upon men? But what has happened? We preach the same old sermons, but Christ is apparently indifferent to them. We go through the same mechanical routine, but there is no stir of life. These many days have passed, and there have been no additions to our church roll. We have won men to ourselves, but not to Christ. And so it seems as though whilst men flattered us, and whilst we had a certain complacency in their applause, heaven passed on unheeding, the souls of men were unreached, and our churches were just dying of inanition; the old passing on to God, but the young untouched, unsaved.

May not the question therefore come to us now, "Perhaps, after all, Christ has ceased to use me! Christ has no further purpose for me! I am too clumsy, too obtuse, too disobedient, too full of myself, too much out of touch with Him! And so I am to be put on the shelf!" Like those great stones in the quarry at Baalbec—almost completely quarried, but yet the temple was finished without them! May not this question go through the audience, "Am I a castaway? I belong to Christ, and when I die I believe I will go home to Him. I know that He has saved me by His precious blood; but has He ceased to use me?"

Look for a moment upon the pages of Scripture, and see how they are

LITTERED WITH CASTAWAYS!

Let us then understand why men are cast away.

I take the first case, that of Esau. He comes in from hunting. He is born to the birthright. The birthright includes the power of standing between God and the clan, speaking to God for men. He is famished. Yonder is the steaming mess of pottage prepared by his brother Jacob.

"Give me that red lentil pottage," he cries.

Jacob, crafty in heart, bargains, "Give me your spiritual birthright."

Is there not here some Christian, who in the past has had some steaming mess of pottage appealing to the senses? There is not one of us who has not been tempted by some temptation to sense. Aye, it may be there is many a man who is glancing back into his past life, and who knows that he has yielded—not once or twice, but oftener —to the appeal to the senses. He has taken a drink, or indulged some other appetite, and has despised his birthright.

I once heard a story that made my heart ache, of a gray-headed man who had been greatly used of God. In his home he had fallen into one gross act of immorality. Another went to accuse him of his crime. They were sitting together at the tea-table. His portion was not sufficiently sweet; and in the midst of this talk upon which depended whether or not the one should be held guilty, and whether he should be permitted to continue in his ministry, he said slightingly, "My tea is sour. Give me some more sugar."

He cared more at that awful moment of his life whether or not the tea was sour or sweet enough, while his power as a minister of God's holy gospel was trembling in the balance. He did eat and drink, and despised his birthright.

Have *you* never eaten and drunken, and despised your birthright? Are you quite sure that some silent and beautiful form has not come into your life and destroyed your heart's true love? Are you quite sure that there is not in you some hungry appetite that has sought satisfaction?

"Give it me. I must have it. I cannot live without it. Even though I have not quite the spiritual power that I had, give it me."

So men despise their birthright still, and they are cast away. Esau became a prince in this world, and the father of a line of dukes, and all the world flattered him and thought him a prosperous and successful man, but God wrote over him the awful epitaph, "This man is a castaway. He did eat and drink, and rose up, and went his way: thus he despised his birthright."

I turn the page of Scripture, and come to the first king of Israel, Saul. A noble man in many respects, he was sent by God to fulfill His mission, but he put a reserve upon his obedience, and told Samuel with a kind of pious blarney, "Blessed be thou of the Lord: I have performed the commandment of the Lord."

The old prophet at that moment detected the lowing of the herd and the bleating of the flock, and said very

significantly, "Performed the commandment of the Lord!
What means then this bleating of the sheep in mine ears
and the lowing of the oxen which I hear?"

I am not here to denounce specific forms of sin. If I
did, the result would be that the people who were not
directly attacked would hold up their umbrellas and let
my words drip upon some others whom they think they
would fit, and they would suppose therefore that they
passed muster. But I am here to bring you face to face
with the eternal God, to lead your consciences before
the great White Throne, and let the light of the eternal
purity of God blaze like a flashlight upon them. It will
be for you to determine if under the profession of obedience there are some flocks and herds that you are reserving
for yourselves. It is possible when you go to a man's
home, or when you even smell his breath, or when you
hear him speak, to know whether or not he has given up
all for God. Some unfortunate sheep starts bleating. Saul
professed obedience, but kept back something for himself;
and God rejected him. He lingered ten years more on the
throne, but he was a castaway. A young David was already
anointed to succeed him.

So when I pass through the Word of God and take case
after case, my heart bleeds and cries out because I know
not who may be here. I would speak with all tenderness
and all pity and all love. I have not come to scathe
anyone. I have not come to denounce. It is because I know
what the horror of that pit is, and what the horror of
being cast away from God's service means, that I now
speak in this way. You expected that I would bring you
a system of spiritual truth,—and I have such a system to
present; you expected that I was going to teach you how

to receive the Holy Ghost of Pentecost, so that every day might be a Pentecost—and I have that blessed message to tell you; but I dare not come to those deep and blessed subjects until I have introduced into your heart a spirit of self-scrutiny and searching, that everyone may ask himself, "Can it be that though I am a minister, or an officer of the church, and bear around the holy elements on Sunday at the Communion service, and give my money to philanthropic objects—can it be that in God's sight I am a castaway?"

Coming out of a meeting recently a brother minister came up to me, took me by the hand, shook it warmly, and said, "I have enjoyed your meeting so much."

Directly he said that I knew that I had failed. When a man says that he has enjoyed a meeting like this, I know that I have not touched him.

You remember when Jacob got down into the Jabbok ford, how beneath those Syrian stars he wrestled with the angel, and the angel with him. Presently the angel put forth his hand and touched the sinew of his strength, and he limped. Do you think it is possible that Jacob could have limped into the camp next morning, and going to his beloved Rachel, have said to her, "O Rachel, we have had a lovely time all night. I have enjoyed it!"

Rather he must have said to her, "I have had a night which has blasted my strength, which has left a scar upon me which I shall carry till I die. O woman, I have fought with the angel of God's love!"

This may be the beginning of

A NEW ERA IN MANY A LIFE.

But we must begin at the bottom; we must begin at the

root of our self-confidence. The prime cause of all failure
in private life as well as in public ministry is the assertion
of self. As long as men and women think it is all right
with them, nothing can be done for them. It is only when
there is excited within them a fear that after all things
may not be quite so well as they seem, a dread that after
all they may have made a mistake and be self-deceived, it
is only then that in the secret of their own chambers they
begin to ask God, "Am I just what I expected?" It is
then that the heart is laid open, and they may be brought
to understand how a man may be almost a castaway and
yet be taken back to the bosom of Christ as Peter was; for
within six weeks the man who was nearly cast away became the Apostle of Pentecost.

Paul said, "Lest I should be a castaway. Therefore,
though I have a perfect right to go to an idol temple, I
shall not go for fear other men seeing me go may follow
me, and what might be innocent to me might be death to
them. Lest I should ruin any man's soul by going, I will
abstain. I have a perfect right, if I choose, to take a wife;
but I shall not do it. I will live a bachelor life, and toil
with my hands, because by being lonesome myself I may
touch some other man who is lonesome too, and by
working with my own hands I shall stay upon the bench
beside others who will be drawn to me by sympathy.
There are many things which this body of mine may have
in innocence, but I shall not take them because I wish to
keep my body under, lest it should master me and cause
me to be a castaway."

Christ waits—the sweet strong, pure Son of God—His
heart yearning over men and yearning to pour itself
through us to save them. But many of us have choked

Him, resisted Him, thwarted Him. One feels like asking the whole audience to fall before Him in confession, and to ask that this holy day may not pass until He has restored us to fellowship with Himself.

My friend, Dr. Harry Grattan Guinness, told me once that all the water supply had become choked out of their college in Derbyshire, England. They could not obtain one drop of water from the bottom to the top of the house. They searched the cisterns, and inspected the taps and the whole machinery, and found no cause. At last they went to the junction between the main reservoir-pipe and their house-pipe, and there in the orifice, in the joint between the two, squatted a huge toad, which (as they were told) had probably come in as a tadpole, had fed upon the water, and had grown to this size, so that the whole water was stopped because it choked the orifice.

Your life has been dry lately; no tear, no prayer, no fervor. You have not met Christ, you have not seen His face for many a long day, He has not used you. It must be because there is something in your heart, innocent once but injurious now. May God show you what it is! Get quiet, and prostrate yourself before God. If people want to speak to you brush past them. If they want to detain you with small talk, leave them. Cast yourself down in some solitary place before God, and say, "May God forgive me! May God show me the sin, show me what it is that hinders me, show me what has nearly wrecked my life. Whatever comes, may I not be a castaway, but still used by Thee through the Holy Ghost for Christ."

"MARRED: SO HE MADE IT AGAIN"

ONCE PAGANNINI, standing before a great audience, broke string after string in his violin, until only one was left. He held up his violin, and said, "One string and Pagannini."

Now we want one man and God; God working through a man so that the man is the channel. But before God can work by a man, he must be right, and I have to speak now on how God can make a man right, fit for service.

In the preceding address we came to despair. We stood upon the brink of the precipice and looked down into the dark, fearing that we might be castaways. Now I take for my text the words:

"He made it again." Jeremiah 18:4.

What did he make again? Jeremiah was a disappointed man. He thought he could do no more to stay the people from destruction. His heart was breaking. God told him to go down to the potter's house, and there he saw the potter take a piece of clay and place it on a wheel. As he stood there to watch, the potter shaped it: it rose beneath his hand into a fair and lovely shape. But just as it was complete, and it seemed as though nothing more was needed, it crumbled beneath his hand. Some part of it fell upon the wheel, some part upon the ground. Jeremiah thought that the potter would take another piece of clay and make that clay fulfill his plan, but instead he stooped and gathered the broken clay with his hand, picked it from the ground, and kneading it with his hand he placed it once more upon the wheel and began to make that clay again; and presently a vessel as fair as possible stood complete, ready to be taken to the kiln to be baked and made permanent.

Away back in your life God took you and placed you upon the wheel, and for these many years God has sought to make you fair. But I know not why, I cannot tell—God knows—you know—there has come a flaw and break, and you are a piece of broken pottery. Your life is a marred life, your ideal a broken ideal, and all around there lie the littered pieces of the man or the woman that you might have been.

But now what shall you do? God put you in that place for a high purpose, but you have missed your mark. Shall God take another man and give him your wealth, another woman and give her your position? Shall God take another student and put him in your church? Shall God call another body to perform the work your church should do? Not yet, not yet. He might take another piece of clay and make that a vessel, but instead He comes again to seek you. His hand is passing through this audience to find you, that the broken pieces of your life, your marred and spoiled ideal, may be made over again. Clergyman, merchant, lady of fashion, Christian worker, student, singer,—God's hand is feeling for you now. The hand of God is, so to speak, laying hold upon the broken pieces of your marred and spoiled life, and if you will let Him, He will now begin to complete your nature by making it to be what He meant it to be years ago when you were cradled at the foot of the cross.

Why have you failed? Because your life *is* a failure. You hide it by going to church, by observing the outward routine, by a hearty laugh, by a light, gay air. You live your life amongst your brethren or sisters, but no one knows that deep down in your soul you are certain that you are a failure, that you are spoiled, that you want things you do not obtain, that you long for a goodness you never realize, that you reach out for a sweetness and purity and strength that never comes. You know that your life has fallen beneath God's plan. You are ready to confess it. Why is it so? Is it because God has failed?

See that mother bending over the cradle where her firstborn babe lies. See how a smile lights up her face as she thinks she catches the plaudits which are to welcome his success in coming years. But no woman ever cherished for her babe visions half so fair as your God has for you. He hates nothing that He has made, and with an equal love He wants to do

HIS BEST FOR EACH.

What then is the cause? Is it that He has made a mistake in your life? You think so. If instead of being a poor man you had been rich, if instead of being a lone woman you had had one to call you wife, and little children to clutch your dress and call you mother; if instead of being tied to the office-stool you had been a minister or missionary, you think that you would have been a better, a sweeter character. But I want you to understand that God chose for you your lot in life out of myriads that were open to Him, because just where you are you might realize your noblest possibilities. Otherwise God would have made you different from what you are. But your soul, born into His kingdom, was a matter of care and thought to Him, how best He might nurture you; and He chose your lot with its irritations, its trials, its difficulties, all the agony that eats out your nature. Though men and women do not guess it, He chose it just as it is, because in it, if you will let Him, He can realize the fairest life within your reach.

Where is the failure? Look. I think I have the wheel before me. My foot is working the treadle. It is revolving rapidly, horizontally as you know. I have placed it on the clay. I begin to manipulate it. It rises beneath my hand till I come to one certain point where, either through some flaw in the clay, a bubble or a fault, it resists me. Leaving that point, I put my hand around again, and in some other direction endeavor to secure my purpose, and then come back to that one point, but again I meet that obstruction that thwarts me. The genius of my brain as an artist is complete; the power of my hand to manipulate is unrivaled; it is *the clay* that thwarts me, until presently, because I have been frustrated again and again, the work is a marred, spoiled thing.

Now is not that true of you?

The one trouble of my life, years ago, was just this about which I am speaking now. God was dealing with me. I suppose He wanted to make me a vessel fit for His use. But there was one point in my life where I fought God as the clay fights the hand of the potter. I fought God, I will not say for how long. God help me! the only benefit that I can get now out of those years the canker-worm has eaten, is to discover the secret in other lives while they too are standing still, and then to take them to the Christ to whom I went myself, and to encourage them to hope that He who years ago took up a spoiled and marred life and made a little of it, will take other men and women and will find out where they have thwarted Him; and finding it out, will touch them there, and as they yield to Him they will be made again.

Now what is the point in your life where you obstruct God? Allow me to search you.

WHERE IS IT?

People come to me and speak of the different points in which they have thwarted God. A man came to me one day and said that when I was in a certain convention I asked all those who wanted to be wholly for God to stand up. He refused to stand, and for months his will rose up and said, "Who is this man that I should stand up when he bids me?"

For months he fought this feeling, until not long ago he came to me and said, "Come and pray! I want to confess that I have been fighting the will of God for months, and I am wretched. Help me to get peace."

I was once staying with another man, a pastor. I had said nothing about smoking—I never do single out sins— I had not alluded to the habit; but one day we were walking along a street that led over a river, and to my surprise as we got to the apex of the bridge he took his tobacco-pouch and pipe and threw them over, and said, "There, I have settled that."

Then, turning to me, he said: "I know, Mr. Meyer, you have said nothing about it; but for the last few months God has been asking me to set a new example to my young men, and I said, 'Why should not I do as I like, and they as they like?' God was searching me, and I was fighting Him; but it is all settled now, sir, it is all done now."

A bright young girl, at the end of one of my addresses, was waiting about, and I said to her:

"Come, my girl, I am quite sure that you have got nothing to see me about."

"O," she said, "I have, sir. I remember that three or four years ago, when I was a girl at school, one of my companions asked me to go out and get some candy for her. I got it, but I kept back half the money for myself. That sin has been working in my mind. It seems as if God keeps saying, 'Confess, confess, restore'; but, sir, I have been fighting it for the last month or two. It looks so stupid to do a little thing like that."

I said, "My dear child, nothing is stupid that is going to please God and put you right with His will."

A man came to me and said, "I cannot understand it, sir, but it seems as if God is blotted out of my life. I used to be so happy."

I said, "How is it?"

Said he, "I think it has to do with my treatment of my brother. He served me cruelly over my father's will, and I said I would never forgive him. I am sorry I said it, but he has been going from bad to worse, has lost his wife and child, and is now on a bed of death, and I cannot go to him because I said I never would."

I said, "My friend, it is better to break a bad vow than keep it. Go."

He went, and the smile of God met him just there. Sixteen years ago I was a minister in a Midland town in England, not at all happy, doing my work for the pay I got, but holding a good position amongst my fellows. Hudson Taylor and two young students came into my life. I watched them. They had something I had not. Those young men stood there in all their strength and joy. I said to Charles Studd, "What is the difference between you and me? You seem so happy, and I somehow am in the trough of the wave."

He replied, "There is nothing that I have got which you may not have, Mr. Meyer."

But I asked, "How am I to get it?"

"Well," he said, "have you given yourself right up to God?"

I winced. I knew that if it came to that, there was a point where I had been fighting my deepest convictions for months. I had lived away from it, but when I came to the Lord's table and handed out the bread and wine, then it met me; or when I came to a convention or meeting of holy people, something stopped me as I remembered this. It was the one point where my will was entrenched. I thought I would do something with Christ that night which would settle it one way or the other, and I met Christ. You will forgive a man who owes everything to one night in his life if to help other men he opens his heart for a moment. I knelt in my room and gave Christ the ring of my will with the keys on it, but kept one little key back, the key of a closet in my heart, in one back story in my heart. He said to me:

"Are they all here?"

And I said, "All but one."

"What is that?" said He.

"It is the key of a little cupboard," said I, "in which

I have got something which Thou needest not interfere with, but it is mine."

Then, as He put the keys back into my hand, and seemed to be gliding away to the door, He said:

"My child, if you cannot trust Me with all, you do not trust Me at all."

I cried, "Stop," and He seemed to come back; and holding the little key in my hand, in thought I said:

"I cannot give it, but if Thou wilt take it Thou shalt have it."

He took it, and within a month from that time He had cleared out that little cupboard of things which had been there for months. I knew He would.

May I add one word more? Three years ago I met the thing I gave up that night, and as I met it I could not imagine myself being such a fool as nearly to have sold my birthright for that mess of pottage.

I looked up into the face of Christ and said, "Now I am thine." It seemed as if that was the beginning of a new ministry. The Lord got me on His wheel again, and He made me again, and He has been making me again ever since. I learned that night to say "yes," and I have tried to say "yes" ever since.

Now, my friend, you say to me, "It is quite true, sir; my life is marred. But I am getting to be an old man. Do you think there is any hope for me?"

My text says: "He made it again."

Adelaide Proctor says, at the end of one of her verses, that we always may be what we might have been. In a sense that is not true. You and I never can recall the past, and yet—and yet Jesus has a wonderful knack of making men again.

There was Jacob, the supplanter, for instance. He met him again at the ford of Jabbok, and he was made into Israel, a prince of God. There was Peter, and He made him again so that on the day of Pentecost he became the means of the Holy Ghost's advent to the world. And He made again John Mark who went back before a touch of seasickness to his mother, but Paul said of him after, "Bring him, for he is profitable." He will make you again.

Canon Wilberforce told me that he had his likeness painted by the great artist Herkomer, who told him the following story. Herkomer was born in the Black Forest, his father a simple woodchopper. When the artist rose to name and fame in London, and built his studio at Bushey, his first thought was to have the old man come and spend the rest of his years with him. He came, and was very fond of molding clay. All day he made things out of clay, but as the years passed he thought his hand would lose its cunning. He often went upstairs at night to his room with the sad heart of an old man who thinks his best days are gone by. Herkomer's quick eye of love detected this, and when his father was safe asleep his gifted son would come down stairs and take in hand the pieces of clay which his old father had left, with the evidences of defect and failure; and with his own wonderful touch he would make them as fair as they could be made by human hand. When the old man came down in the morning, and took up the work he had left all spoiled the night before, and held it up before the light, he would say, rubbing his hands, "I can do it as well as ever I did."

Is not that just what God Almighty is going to do with you? You are bearing the marks of failure just because you have been resisting Him and fighting Him. But, ah!

my Lord comes with those pierced hands, and says, "Will you not yield to me? Only yield, and I will make you again."

There is a Pentecost for us all, but we must begin at the beginning. There must be the yielding.

Young girls who have come out of beautiful homes, the children of luxury, I tell you that all the exterior beauty of your life is only a faint adumbration and shadow of the infinite sweetness and grace of the life of Pentecost. Live in the promised land, men and women, you who have been seeking in the outside, in circumstances and things and people, your bliss.

YOU HAVE MISSED IT

—you always will that way. It is inside. It is in the Holy Ghost. It is in Christ. Heaven is there. It is there for all. But believe me, you cannot get it unless you take the preparatory step. Therefore you must get alone as I did sixteen years ago; you must kneel down before Christ and say:

"Christ, I give Thee my self, my will. With my will I yield to Thee. Thou art the Potter; I am the clay. Impose Thy will upon me."

And mind you, Christ will say to you, "What about this?" and if you can look up and say; "Yes, that is Thine," He will go forward and make you beautiful and happy. But if you refuse, you will stop there, you will be dwarfed, you will thwart Christ.

At Keswick, a little village in the Cumberland Hills, where we meet once a year to talk about these things, if you go out at ten o'clock, at eleven o'clock, at twelve o'clock, at one o'clock at night, you will see lights burning.

My heart has often gone up in prayer because I know that every light means a Jabbok, and that at those places souls are yielding to God. At Northfield also a brother clergyman said to me, "Mr. Meyer, the work has not been done in the auditorium, but it has been done in the woods at night where we have gone to settle it with God."

Remember this. When I gave myself to God that night, the devil said, "Don't do it! If you let God have an inch, He will want an ell. If you yield in one thing you will have to yield in everything, and there is no knowing what you may not come to."

At first I thought there was something in it. Then I remembered my daughter, who was a little willful then, and loved her own way. I thought to myself as I knelt, "Supposing that she were to come and say— 'Father, from to-night I am going to put my life into your hand; do with it what you will.' Would I call her mother to my side and say: 'Here is a chance to torment her. What would mortify her? what color dress does she hate? what companion does she detest? what method of spending her life does she abhor? Tell me, and I will put her through them all.' "

I knew I would not say that. I knew I would say to my wife, "Our child is going to follow our will from now. Do you know of anything that is hurting her?"

"Yes; so and so."

"Does she love it much?"

"Yes."

"Ah! she must give it up, but we will make it as easy for her as we can. We must take from her the things that are hurting her, but we will give her everything that will make her life one long summer day of bliss."

God will say that to you. He only takes that one thing away because it will hurt you. But oh! He will give, and give, and give! You have no idea what God will do for you. Say: "I am willing." But let me make a confession: I did not say that myself. I said, "I am not willing, O God, but I am willing to be made willing."

God help you to make the same prayer!

THE NATURAL MAN

IF IT WERE NOT that I believe in the Holy Ghost, I would almost shrink from speaking about the profound philosophy wherewith the apostle Paul deals with the self-life; but I believe that God's Spirit will take my broken words and speak to each of you.

Will you turn to I Corinthians 2:14: "The natural man receiveth not the things of the Spirit of God: for they are foolishness unto him: neither can he know them, because they are spiritually discerned."

"The natural man." The Greek is the "psychical" man, the man in whom the soul is all, and the spirit is like a dark, untenanted chamber.

The temple of old was constituted thus: outer court, holy place, holy of holies. The outer court corresponds to our body, the holy place to our soul, the holy of holies or the most holy place to our spirit. In the regenerate man the most holy place is tenanted by the Spirit of God, but in the unregenerate man it is untenanted and dark, waiting for its occupant. The natural man is the man whose spirit is empty of God.

In the fifteenth verse of the same chapter, we read: "But he that is spiritual judgeth all things, yet he himself is judged of no man."

Here we have the "spiritual" man, the man whose

spirit is quick with the Spirit of God, who speaks and wills and lives beneath the impulse of the Holy Ghost Himself. Oh, that every believer became truly spiritual; spirit-unfilled (written with a small "s"): the Spirit of God (written with a large "S") dominating the spirit of man.

In the third chapter of the same epistle, Paul begins, "And I, brethren, could not speak unto you as unto spiritual, but as unto carnal, even as unto babes in Christ."

Now the "carnal" man is a Christian, a babe in Christ. We might think that the carnal man is unregenerate, but it is not so. He is regenerate, he is in Christ, and Christ is in him; but instead of Christ being predominant, the carnal element is predominant. I believe that there are hundreds of people who are in Christ; but they are babes in Christ. Christ is in them, but He is overcrowded by the superiority of their self-life. Their self-life was once clothed in rags; it is now clothed in the externals of religion; but it is still the self-life, and in the Christian may predominate over the Christ-life, and be the cause of unutterable darkness and sorrow.

May God help me now to reverse it, so that the carnal element shall be crowded out, shall be crucified, and the Christ element shall become the pivot of your life!

In order that you may know what the carnal element is, let me say that that word also stands for "flesh," and that the Greek word is sarx ($\sigma\acute{\alpha}\rho\xi$). Now the Apostle uses the word "flesh," "carnal," or "sarx" in a very especial form. He does not mean the natural body, but he means the element of self. That is proved from Romans 7:18, where he says, "In me, (that is, in my flesh), dwelleth no good thing." My flesh is "me." Some men spell it with a tiny *m*, and some with a capital *M*, but whether the *m* is in italics or in capitals, the "me" in each person is the flesh. Spell "flesh" backwards, drop the *h*, as we are apt to do in London, and you get s-e-l-f; "flesh" is "self," and "self" is "flesh." It is "me," and as long as "me" is first and Christ second, I am living a carnal life though I am in Christ and a saved man.

FOUR CHARACTERISTICS OF THE CARNAL LIFE

Now the carnal life is *a babe life*. What is sweeter than a babe? So beautiful, so wee, one can take the child so close to oneself. But what is tender and beautiful in a babe for a few months is terrible at the end of twelve months, or ten years. And what is lovely in a young convert is terrible in a man of ten or twenty years of Christian life. I have met men who use the same expressions twenty years after conversion that they did when they were cradled on Calvary; and if you are still living in the elementary stage of experience and feeling and prayer, and do not grow, do not know God better, do not know the Bible better, do not know yourself better, do not know Christ better, you are a little babe, you are carnal.

And then the carnal man *lives on milk*. Paul said, "I have fed you with milk, and not with meat: for hitherto ye were not able to bear it, neither yet now are ye able." Milk is food which has passed through the digestion of another. The babe cannot take meat, so the mother takes meat, and breaks it down, and the child takes milk. So many Christians cannot read the Bible, cannot get any good out of the Bible, it must be broken down by their minister, and they are fed with a spoon! Ministers are nurses. They have to spend their time wheeling the converts about, comforting them, putting them to sleep, waking them up and feeding them; and if they are not fed with a spoon three or four times a week, there is no knowing what will happen. And if you are in that state that you must take spiritual truth through the digestion of another, you are a babe.

A carnal Christian is also *sectarian*. "I am of Paul, and I am of Apollos, and I of Cephas." Oh, how much we make of the fold, and how little of the flock! How much we think of the hurdles, and how little of the sheep! One man says, "I am a Baptist"; and another, "I am a Presbyterian"; a third says, "I am a Roman Catholic"; and a fourth, "I am evangelical." Half the time we are worrying about the sect to which we belong. Directly a man begins in that course, and forgets the Church with a large C— the Church of Christ—he is a carnal Christian and a babe.

I would lead you one step further because I desire to make my system perfectly clear. Turn to Hebrews 5:14, where we read:

"Strong meat belongeth to them that are of full age, even those who by reason of use have their senses exercised to discern both good and evil."

Here we have a fourth characteristic of the carnal Christian: such an one is *unable to exercise his senses to discern good and evil*. When I returned to England from one of my Atlantic voyages, my nose was very sensitive: the pure ozone of the Atlantic had made me very keen to discern impurity. I went to stay with some friends in the country, and all that time I was haunted by a noisome effluvia. I said, "What is the matter?"

"Oh," they said, "there is nothing wrong."

I said, "I am sure there is," and presently, after investigating, about a mile off we discovered a sewage-farm which infected the air. My friends who had had no training on the Atlantic were unable to detect it. So there are men who take up a novel full of impure thought and read it and not feel hurt, though the hurt has been certainly received; men and women who listen to uncharitable talk, and not detect its undertone; men and women who go in and out in the world and mix in its pleasure and sin, and still call themselves Christians, because they cannot discern good and evil.

Those four tests,—are they true of you? I am here as a surgeon, and must help you to anatomize yourself to know where you are. Are you growing? Are you living on the strong meat of the Bible? Are you a sectary? Have you the power to discriminate between good and evil? By these four tests you may know whether the Christ-life or the flesh-life is predominant in you.

Let us go deeper. When God created man, He gave all intelligent beings a self-hood, a power of self-determination. He gave it to angels. Demons have it, because they were angels. Men have it—selfhood. The Creator meant the selfhood to be dependent on Himself, so that a Christian might turn to the Creator and say, "Live Thou in Thy will through me." When Jesus Christ, the perfect man, came among men, during all His earthly life He said nothing and willed nothing from Himself; He lived a truly dependent life. The vegetable creation— flowers, the trees—they depend on God absolutely, and that makes them so beautiful. Consider the lilies and the cedars, how they grow! And the angels who have kept their first estate live on God. God wills, thinks, acts, energizes through them. Satan was once an archangel dependent on God, but something passed over him and he caught the fever of independence, and began to make himself his own pivot; and so he began to be in hell; because hell is the assertion of self to the exclusion of God, and heaven is the assertion of God to the exclusion of self. The devil fell, and all his crew that leaned on him, instead of on God, fell also. Then when man was made, Satan traversed the abyss, and whispered to man, "Be God, be independent, take your own way, do your own will."

Man in his fall withdrew his nature from dependence upon God, and made himself a center of his own life and activity. And this world is cursed to-day because men and women are living for self, and the flesh-life. The carnal mind is enmity against God, and is darkness and despair.

Christianity is a science, a deep science, which tries to do away with the evil or the fall into selfishness by substituting for self the Son of God, which is Christ. Is it not wonderful that Hindooism and Christianity are each of them intended to deal with the same root of evil? But the Hindoo tries to exterminate the self-life by absorption in eternity until Nirvana sets in, while the Christian who also sees that the self-life is accursed eliminates it by the philosophy and the action which I am now going to describe.

SELF-WILL SHOWS ITSELF IN VARIOUS FORMS

"Now the works of the flesh are manifest, which are these: Adultery, fornication, uncleanness, lasciviousness, idolatry, witchcraft, hatred, variance, emulations, wrath, strife, seditions, heresies, envyings, murders, drunkenness, revelings, and such like." There you have the passion of the self-life in lust. "Are ye so foolish? having begun in the Spirit are ye now made perfect by the flesh?" There you have the aspirations of the self-life, trying to perfect itself. There was a school of perfection in Galatia, and they sought to perfect themselves in their own energy; and there have been schools of perfection since then which have tried to be good in the energy of the self-life. "Let no man beguile you of your reward in a voluntary humility and worshiping of angels, intruding into those things which he hath not seen, vainly puffed up by his fleshly mind, and not holding the Head, from which all the body by joints and bands having nourishment ministered, and knit together, increaseth with the increase of God." There you have some intellectualism prying into the things of God, but not submitting to the will of God and the teaching of God. "When I therefore was thus minded, did I use lightness? or the things that I purpose, do I purpose according to the flesh, that with me there should be yea, yea, and nay, nay?" There you have the self-life planning, scheming, and arranging for itself, and the Apostle says: "I am not going to plan after the flesh."

We see then that we are always in danger of doing good things from the self pivot. That is our curse. I hear of a man who has consecrated himself to God, and I say to myself: "I will do the same." I hear of a man who has attracted crowds by some special lantern, or by some new machinery, and I say: "I too will do the same." I learn of a school which is teaching a certain line of doctrine, and because I think it will pay, and get me prestige and popularity I adopt it. But not until I begin to notice the working of my own life, shall I have any conception how perpetually the self-life is underlying all.

HOW TO GET RID OF THE SELF-LIFE

I will show you. There are *three steps:* the cross, the Spirit, the contemplation of the risen Christ. May we take them now; may the Spirit of God reveal to each one this blessed secret!

First, the cross. Now understand that I hold that on the cross Jesus Christ offered a substitutionary sacrifice for the sins of the whole world. But there is a second meaning significant in the cross. Turn to Romans 8:3, 4: "What the law could not do in that it was weak through the flesh, God sending His own Son in the likeness of sinful flesh, and for sin, condemned sin in the flesh: that the righteousness of the law might be fulfilled in us, who walk not after the flesh but after the Spirit." God sent His own Son in the likeness of sinful flesh, and for sin. "For sin" is substitutionary. "In the likeness of sinful flesh" is the reference of the cross to sanctification. On the cross God nailed in the person of Christ the likeness of our sinful flesh. I cannot explain it to you more than that; but I know this—that next to seeing Jesus as my sacrifice, nothing has revolutionized my life like seeing the effigy of my sinful self in the sinless, dying Saviour. I say to myself:

"God has nailed the likeness of my self-life to the cross. The cross is the symbol of degradation and curse. Cursed is everyone that hangs on the cross. If then God has treated the likeness of my sinful self, when borne by the sinless Christ, as worthy of His curse, how terrible in

God's sight it must be for myself to hug it and embrace it and live in it!"

Oh, wondrous cross! But that is not all.

Christ and I are one. In Him I hung there. I came to an end of myself in Christ, and kneeling at His cross I took the position of union with Him in His death, and I consigned my self-life to the cross. It was as though I took my self-life with its passions, its choices, its yearnings after perfection, its wallowing, its fickleness, its judgment of others, its uncharity—I took it as a felon, and said:

"Thou art cursed, thou shalt die. My God nailed thee to that cross. Come, thou shalt come. I put thee there by my choice, by my will, by my faith. Hang there."

After that moment—you remember in Galatians it is the aorist tense: "They that are Christ's, crucified the flesh with its affections and lusts"—after that moment, that decisive in my life, I have ever reckoned that my self-life is on the cross, and that the death of Christ lies between me and it.

Let me make that perfectly clear. Supposing a woman has been married to a felon, a drunkard, a libertine. After years of sorrow there comes a moment of liberty when she seeks and obtains a divorce. She now enters into union with a perfectly lovely blessed man who becomes to her everything. Whenever her former husband reels along the street and seeks again to get her back into his power, she points to a moment, the moment when the divorce was granted, and she says, "From that moment I became divorced from you. Touch me if you dare."

If he comes reeling across the street, she only clutches closer the arm of the true man she loves, and puts him on the other side between the sot and herself. She counts from the moment of deliverance.

Now think about it, pray about it. Later I am going to publish the marriage-bans between you and Christ, and to show how Christ takes the place of self. But we must move together, my friends. You must allow me to be persistent. You will not benefit by this teaching unless you act as the result of any separate address in the direction it indicates. So kneel down before the cross of Jesus, and realize why your Christian life has been a failure. The cause of your darkness and sorrow and desertion is to be found here: you have never consigned the self-life where God consigned it. In your will, with streaming eyes, with reverent face, unite yourself with the death of Christ. Doing so, remember you will do what Jesus said Peter must do. Peter said, "Thou art the Christ."

"Well and good," Christ replied. "I am going to die."

Peter said, "You must not think of it. Spare Thyself."

Ah, that is what you will hear said to you a thousand times—spare thyself!

Jesus said, "Get thee behind me. That is Satan: it is the spirit of the pit. If a man will come after me, let him deny himself, and take up his cross and follow me."

You may say what you like about Christianity, but I undertake to affirm it has been shamefully misrepresented, both by Protestant and by any other class of Christians. They have thought that Christianity depended in the objective, whereas it is subjective largely, equally. They have thought that it depended on trusting Christ to put away your sin, whereas it also consists in trusting Christ to deliver you from yourselves, who are the center and curse of your life.

Whenever the self-life obtrudes, reckon yourself dead to it; reckon that the cross stands between you and it.

But you say, "Sir, I do not see how I am to live like that. I shall always be on pins and needles, always in agony whether this is self or not, and I do not see how I am to live."

Ah, I thought you would say that! I said that myself, and here comes the *second* point: the Holy Spirit.

"If ye through the Spirit do mortify the deeds of the body, ye shall live." And again, "The Spirit lusteth against the flesh."

It was by the Eternal Spirit that Christ offered Himself without spot to God, and it is by the Eternal Spirit that the cursed spirit of self is going to be antagonized in your life and mine. Just as in a scarlet-fever case you use carbolic acid, and the carbolic acid antagonizes the germs of disease, so turning from that curse I kneel before the Holy Ghost, and say, "Spirit of God, infill, *infill,* INFILL my entire being, deeper, deeper, deeper yet. In the depth of my nature, when I am least thinking about it, go on day by day as the antiseptic of my flesh or self-life. Antagonize it, work against it, keep it out of sight, keep it under Christ."

The Holy Ghost will do it.

But you say, "Mr. Meyer, I am so afraid that if I am always dealing with the self-life, it will hurt me. It will be like standing by a bier and seeing death disintegrate a corpse."

This leads me to my *third* point, and I reply—and this is the beauty of it—that while the Spirit of God in the depth of your heart is antagonizing the self-life, He does it by making Jesus Christ a living, bright reality. He fixes

your thoughts upon Jesus. You do not think about the
Spirit, you hardly think about self, but you think much
about your dear Lord; and all the time that you are
thinking about Him, the process of disintegration and
dissolution and death of self is going on within your
heart.

A dear sister said to me once, "I am going to spend a
whole day praying for the Holy Ghost."

She went to a hut in a wood, and she came back to me
at night and said, "I have had a grand day, but I am a
bit disappointed. I do not feel that I have more of the
Holy Ghost now than I did."

"But," I said, "is Jesus much to you?"

"Oh," she replied, "Jesus never was so sweet and
precious as He is now."

"Why, my dear woman," I said, "that is the Holy Ghost,
because He glorifies Christ, and when the Holy Ghost
works most, you do not think about the Holy Ghost, but
you think about your dear Lord."

O, man and woman, forgive me! It is a very broken,
broken way of putting the deepest mystery in the Bible,
but I can only ask that the Holy Spirit may make you
know what it is to have Jesus as the center and origin of
your life. The fountain and origin hitherto has been self,
has it not? O cursed self, Barabbas, Barabbas, to the cross!
The world says: "Not Christ, but Barabbas, self." The
Christian says: "Not Barabbas, but Christ."

May God explain this to you, for His name's sake.

THE SUBSTITUTION OF THE
CHRIST-LIFE FOR THE SELF-LIFE

IN MY SECOND ADDRESS we saw that the will is our main and chief impediment. We are not what we *feel,* or *think,* or *wish,* but what we *will.* In the preceding address we saw that our curse lies in making self the pivot of our life, and that the one aim of Christianity is to put Christ where man puts self. I want now to show shortly, concisely, with the power of God's Spirit who coöperates, how this may be done, and I am going to use the Epistle to the Galatians.

In Galatians 5:19, we have the works of self: "Adultery, fornication, uncleanness, lasciviousness, idolatry, witchcraft, hatred, variance, emulations, wrath, strife, seditions, heresies, envyings, murders, drunkenness, revelings, and such like." Wherever man's nature works itself out, the lust of the flesh shows itself in every casino, saloon and house of ill-fame.

Turn to Galatians 3:3: "Are ye so foolish? Having begun in the Spirit, are ye now made perfect by the flesh?" Will you be made perfect in the flesh? In the regenerate man, the church-member, there is the same principle of self-life; and though you do not find him in a den of drink or lust or infamy, the same principle which is working unrestrained and unbridled there is working in his heart also. He gives to the collection, to the subscription list, that men may see how much he gives. He seeks to please God by prayer, by the communion, by ritualistic observances. He will even try to be perfect. There is many a man who goes to Keswick and to Northfield, trying to pile up his religious life in the energy of his religious-looking self. But I repeat it: the curse of the Christian and of the world is that self is our pivot; it is because Satan made self his pivot that he became a devil. Take heaven from its center in God, and try to center it in self, and you transform heaven into hell. I know little or nothing about the fire, or the darkness, or the worm of hell. Hell is selfishness, and selfishness is hell. And

THE PHILOSOPHY OF THE BIBLE

is to do away with self, and to make Christ all in all.

When I am dealing with a drunkard I am inclined to say to him, "Be a man."

What a fool I am! I am trying to cast out the evil of drink by the evil of self-esteem. If I want to save a man, I must cast out the spirit of self, and substitute the Lord Jesus Christ. Alpha, Omega, all in all.

But how? How?

This epistle to the Galatians is my battle-axe. Luther used it for justification, but I think it is for sanctification.

How? By the cross, and by the cross as presented in the Epistle to the Galatians.

The Apostle tells us in Galatians 1:4: "Jesus Christ, who gave Himself for our sins, that He might deliver us from this present evil world, according to the will of God and our Father." He considers the cross in its aspect toward sanctification. He says: "He delivered us from this present evil world." In Romans we have the cross for justification, the putting-away of sin; in Galatians for sanctification, the cross standing between me and my past, between me and the world, between me and myself: the cross, and I count from that cross. That is the ground taken in Galatians.

Take Galatians 2:20: "I have been crucified with Christ." God demands that every man and woman should unite with the cross, and (so to speak) kill the self-life, the egotism, the personal element which has been so strong in each one. Not your individuality, however. Isaiah will still be Isaiah, and Malachi, Malachi; but the proud, fussy self-esteem, yourself, ego, the flesh, must be crucified. Christ denied His divine self, and you and I must deny our fallen self. Christ's temptation was to use His divine attribute; your temptation is that you should use your human attribute. You must put it to the cross, and believe that from this moment it shall be crucified to you and you to it. Barabbas to the cross, to the cross! Christ, come down from the cross and live in here!

Galatians 5:24: The aorist: "They that are Christ's crucified the flesh." Galatians 6:14: "God forbid that I should glory save in the cross of our Lord Jesus Christ, by whom the world is crucified unto me, and I unto the world." The world looks at me as a felon, but I have my revenge. That by which I am crucified to the world, by that the world is crucified to me. It may say what it likes about me. I retaliate, "Take it back; it is all true of thyself."

This wonderful epistle speaks of the cross as between me and Egypt, between me and the wilderness, between me and my past, my wanderings; and now the cross is my

Jordan by which I pass through death into the land where Joshua leads, the land that flows with milk and honey.

This epistle also treats of the Holy Ghost, because as I have said before, it is only the Holy Spirit that can make your reckoning true. You choose the cross, but the Holy Spirit as it were mortifies, makes dead, makes real. *You* reckon, *He* makes real your reckoning. And hence Galatians 5:17: "The flesh lusteth against the Spirit, and the Spirit against the flesh: and these are contrary the one to the other: so that ye cannot do the things that ye would." Galatians 5:16: "*Walk* in the Spirit"; 5:18: "*Be led of* the Spirit"; 5:25: "*Live* in the Spirit." And while you walk in the Spirit, are led of the Spirit, and live in the Spirit, the Holy Spirit will go on lusting and agonizing and making real to you your reckoning of death.

You have not therefore got to worry about the death side; think about the life side. Do not live looking at the corpse, but live looking to the Holy Ghost; and as you trust Him for every movement, as you breath in the Holy Ghost moment by moment as you breathe in air, in the depth of your heart He will draw you away from the flesh, the self, the world, the devil; and insensibly, unconsciously, exquisitely, He will bring you into life. And the more you live on the life side, the more, without knowing much of it, you will live on the death side; for while you are engrossed with the Holy Ghost, the Holy Ghost in the depth of your being is carrying the sentence of death deeper, deeper, deeper down, and things are being mortified of which you once had no conception.

Now listen: If you choose the cross, if you live in the Spirit, the Spirit lusts (always the present tense), lusteth against the flesh. I do not know how your Bible reads, but some Bibles are printed wrong. "The flesh lusteth against the Spirit, and the Spirit against the flesh," and "Spirit" is spelled with a small *s*. Take some ink and alter that. It is not "spirit" with a small *s;* it is "Spirit" with a capital *S,* the Holy Spirit. "The flesh, the self, lusts against the Holy Spirit, and the Holy Spirit lusts against the flesh."

Now, let us look at *five texts in Galatians* on the inner life, the indwelling of Christ.

1. Galatians 1:15, 16: "When it pleased God, who separated me from my mother's womb, and called me by His grace, to reveal His Son in me, that I might preach Him among the heathen; immediately I conferred not with flesh and blood." "It pleased God to reveal His Son in me." Now, "to reveal" means "to undrape." There is a statue. It is covered with a veil. It is there, but hidden. I take off the veil, and you see it. When you were regenerate, Christ came unto you; that is what regeneration means—Christ born into your spirit. But Christ came in as a veiled figure, and you who are regenerate but who have never seen the Christ as I put Him before you in the last address, you have Christ in you, but He is veiled. Now, mark. When Jesus died, the veil of the temple was rent in twain from the top to the bottom; and when the soul appreciates the death of Christ as its own death to sin, the veil is rent in twain from the top to the bottom, and the Holy Ghost reveals Jesus as the Substitute for the self-life.

"It pleased God to reveal His Son in me." O, my God, I thank Thee that Thou hast revealed Thy Son as the Alpha, the pivot, the fountain, the origin of my life! May it be so with us all!

A friend of mine was staying near Mont Blanc. He had

been there for a fortnight, but had not seen the "monarch of the Alps." Nearly out of heart with waiting, he was preparing to leave. Going up to dress for dinner, he passed a window and saw that the monarch was still veiled in mist. Having dressed, he came downstairs, passing the window again. Every vestige of mist had now parted, and Mont Blanc stood revealed from base to snow-clad peak. So now there shall come upon you a breath of the Holy Ghost, before which the misconception of your life shall pass, and to you God will reveal His Son in you as the center of your life.

Turn for a moment to Colossians 1:27, a very favorite passage: "To whom God would make known what is the riches of the glory of this mystery among the Gentiles; which is Christ in you, the hope of glory."

A woman sits alone. Her son ran away to sea twenty years ago. She is a widow, poor, lonely. A bronzed stranger comes.

"Can I sleep in your spare room?"

"I have a room to let, so you can stay."

He comes in disguised, so that she cannot see him. He is there, but she knows him not. One day they sit together at dinner, and there is a gesture, and she says, "John!"

That is the glory of the mystery when the two kiss.

"My boy!"

"My mother!"

Then after dinner he says: "Mother, you shall never lack again. Here is gold. I am going to live with you, never to go away again."

That is the riches of the glory of the mystery of her boy in the house.

Jesus, come! You have come, but You are a mystery. But we have come to the cross, and the mystery is gone, and there is the glory of the day; but there will be the riches of the glory of the mystery, Christ in us; and He will do for us better than ever we could have done for ourselves.

2. Galatians 1:24: "They glorified God in me." Some young men belonging to the Salvation Army came to old Andrew Bonar and said, "Dr. Bonar, we have been all night with God. Can't you see our faces shine?"

The old man said, "Moses wist not that his face shone."

When you have got the real article you do not need to advertize it, the public will come for it; but the man who has got what we call in England, brummagem ware, a sham, must puff it. If you have got Christ in you, people will not glorify you, they will glorify Christ in you, and they will say, "Teach us about Christ who has made you so fair."

"They glorified God in me." Dear brother ministers, when you get this, they will not glorify your sermons, they will not glorify your intellect, and they will not glorify your eloquence; but they will glorify God who shines through you as the Shekinah shone through the temple of old.

3. Galatians 2:8: "The same was mighty in me." Hudson Taylor told me that on the threshold of his great life-work God came to him and said, "My child, I am going to evangelize inland China, and if you like to walk with me I will do it through you."

"Mighty in me." I cannot take that Bible class, but Christ is in me, and HE can. I cannot conduct that mission, but Christ is in me, and HE can. I cannot assume these responsibilities, but hallelujah! it does not matter. A copper wire has only to convey the message, it is for the battery to send it; and you may be forever more like the wire which connects you with cities far down its course, the wire along which the fair and the false passes without fret, without anxiety, without care; a mighty, mighty force meeting in the wire. When it is not self but Christ, it is Christ "mighty in me."

4. Galatians 2:20: "Christ liveth in me." One day when traveling by train, a young man sat opposite me in the car, reading Thomas à Kempis' *Imitation of Christ*. I knew the book, and sat beside him and said, "A grand book."

He said, "Yes."

Said I, "I have found something better."

"Better?"

"Yes."

"How?"

"Better for me, because I was always a poor hand at imitation. I imitated the minister with whom I settled from college, and nobody but myself and my wife ever guessed that my sermons were imitations of his. When I was a boy, my father had me taught drawing, and my master put before me something, and my copy needed to have letter-press underneath to state it was an imitation of the copy. And when I sat down to imitate Christ, no one could have guessed what I was trying to attain. But," said I, "my young friend, if my drawing-master could have infused the spirit of his skill into my brain and hand, he could have drawn through me as fair a drawing as his own; and if my great and noble friend could have only put his spirit into me, why should I not have spoken even as he? And if instead of imitating Christ far away in the glory, He will come by the Holy Ghost and dwell in me, by His grace He shall work through my poor yielded life, a life something like His own fair life." Christ liveth in me.

Many have no idea what religion is. Re-ligion, *re-ligo,* a Latin word meaning "I bind,"—it is the binding of the heart to the Lord. No, I recall that; it is better: "He that is joined to the Lord is one spirit." O Christ, Thou art one with me, to make me one with Thee world without end!

5. One verse more. Galatians 4:19: "My little children, of whom I travail in birth again until Christ be formed in you." You know, of course, that an egg has in it a little embryo of life, and the nutriment the viscous fluid upon which it shall grow; and every day the little life germ pecks into this more and more, and the chick is formed in the shell. Until now there has been a good deal more of other elements in your life than of Christ, but from now the Christ is going to grow and increase and absorb into Himself everything else, and be formed in you.

Brother ministers, will you forgive that I have stated the truths of Christ's holy gospel so imperfectly? How can human words tell what Christ is prepared to be? But let me entreat you to pass by a great deal of political life, and it may be, (though it is not wrong), of the social life around you; and I charge you to live to preach the deep philosophy of the indwelling Christ, and let men know what Jesus meant when He said, "In that day ye shall know that I am in the Father, and ye in me, and I in you."

CHRIST THE COMPLEMENT OF OUR NEED

W E HAVE NOW DEALT with the will, and have seen that our curse is the self-life. We have also learned that Jesus Christ can take the place of self. I want now to show what Jesus Christ can be, and may the Holy Spirit glorify Christ!

I Corinthians 10:11: "Now all these things happened unto them for ensamples: and they are written for our admonition, upon whom the ends of the world are come."

Once we were in Egypt. Everyone who has been redeemed by the blood of Christ was once in Egypt. Egypt stands for three things: (1) sensual pleasure, leeks, garlics, onions; (2) bondage, the taskmaster, the brick, and the treasure city; and (3) anguish of soul. I suppose there is not one now in Christ that does not remember the sensual pleasure, the bondage and the anguish of soul. Out of that God has brought us. He brought us when He brought Christ through death to resurrection, and He brought us when each one (as it were) was sheltered beneath the Paschal Lamb, and the blood spoke to God. O blessed moment when we entered into peace, when we put the blood upon the door-post and the lintel, and because God saw the blood we were ransomed, and in joy went forth from the land of bondage! And as we stood upon the further shore of the Red Sea we repeated Miriam's Song, we rejoiced in God our Saviour. We gave ourselves up to follow the cloud, we sheltered beneath it by day and by night. We depended upon God for everything —for the water that gushed from the rock, and the manna that fell upon the desert floor. O happy, happy, happy days when we, fresh redeemed and with the consciousness of liberty, walked with God in the first hours of our conversion!

Then we came beneath Sinai. We obtained a new thought of God's holiness and righteousness, and as we first came there we said with all the fervor of a true intention: "Whatever God says, we will do." But our joy began to pass away, for as we tried to keep the law of God we fell hour by hour into sin that we loathed. It was the experience of the seventh chapter of Romans. After the inward man we loved the law of God, but when we came to do what we would we found we could not. We were like men raised from some illness, who know how to walk perfectly well, but when they begin they totter, and presently fall to the ground.

After staying there, we heard the command of God to arise and depart, and after some days we came to Kadesh-barnea. Now Kadesh is on the frontier of the land of Canaan. At Kadesh the rolling prairie sinks into the sand and waste of the desert. At Kadesh you looked back on Egypt, and forward into Palestine. To Kadesh there came spies, bringing in their hands baskets full of fruit which they had gathered in the Land of Promise, grapes, pomegranates, apricots, sweet and luscious fruit. At Kadesh you passed them round, you ate, you said, "It is a good land."

Many of you have been to Kadesh. You took lodgings there—at Northfield, at Keswick conventions; and men who have been over into the Land of Promise came back, and in their addresses and books they gave you a basket of fruit, and you said: "It is very good."

But there you stopped, and instead of going over the frontier and living in the land, you have gone

BACK TO THE DESERT.

Why did Israel stop there? Because she did not believe God. She believed that God could bring her from Egypt, but she could not believe that God could bring her to Canaan. She believed in the God of the past, but she could not believe in the God of every moment. She had an evil heart of unbelief, and departed from the living God.

You believe in Calvary, but not in the ascension. You believe in Christ who died, but not in Christ who rose and lives. You believe in conversion as a past fact, but you have no idea that He who converted you is prepared hour by hour to bring you into and to keep you in the Land of Rest.

The wilderness stands for three things.

First. Restlessness; a redeemed people, but restless. There is a chapter in Numbers, and thirty-three times in it we are told that the people removed. That has been your life for years, to and fro, trying this church and that, this minister and that minister, but all the while certain that you have not got God's rest.

Secondly. It stands for discontent; they murmured. And what a murmuring life yours is! You have got riches, love, happy, happy surroundings, but there is always something that you want altered. Discontent! If it is summer, it is too hot. If it is winter, it is too cold. If you have love you want money, and if you have money you want love. Backwards and forwards, full of restless murmuring and discontent. That has been your life as a Christian.

Thirdly. It stands for back-yearning, yearning backwards. The people had come out of Egypt, but they were always thinking about it. And your life is a negative life. You are out of Egypt, but you go as near Egypt as you can, and you look over into the pleasures of Egypt, you look over into the doings of Egypt, you look over into the passions and sins of Egypt, and though you are out of it your heart hungers after it. You are a Christian, but a worldly man has a happier time than you, for the worldly man has never had a glimpse of what you have. He is contented. You have enough religion to make you wretched.

What next? You came to Jordan. The poet has taught us to think that Jordan means death, the death of the body; but that is a false conception. In God's imagery the Jordan stands for death, but not the death of the body, but death to the self-life. I trust I have made it clear that I do not believe that self ever dies. I do not believe in the eradication of self, but I believe we come to the cross, to Jordan, and we put the cross, the death of Christ, between ourselves and our past life. We pass through the Jordan in our own experience when we unite ourselves with Christ's death, and are planted with Him in the likeness of His death. After that we stand in the land of Canaan.

At Kadesh you looked over, but now you are in. You do not feel much. When you awoke you thought you would feel joy, but it is not so. You are quiet and still. Never mind! A man may cross the equator and not know it. The equator is marked on the map, but not on the ocean, and a man may cross it and not know it. Without emotion or passion, relying upon the Holy Ghost to make your reckoning true, you have passed Jordan, you are now in the land.

AND WHAT IS THE LAND?

The land is Christ. Canaan is Christ. He is the Land of Promise. Those mountains are the mountains of His strength. Those valleys are His humility. Those springs are His joy. Those rivers are His Holy Spirit. Those treasures are His wealth. That land—look at it! It is all yours. It is Christ in you, and you in Christ—that is Paradise.

That is proved by Hebrews 3:14: "We are made partakers of Christ." The third chapter of Hebrews is the wilderness experience. The fourth chapter is the Christ possession; and the Apostle says that we who believe are made to partake of Christ. Christ in us, Christ around us, Christ in the glory! I want to talk to you about that.

The first thing to do is to *get to know the land.* I remember when I was in Chicago someone told me that a family may purchase, or obtain from your Government, a farm in the far West. Gathering their goods together, a father, mother, and children will travel in the caravan (as we would call it in England), to the far West. They will sit in their house on the edge of their inheritance while the father surveys it. Leaving his wife and children, he climbs the mountain, and looks that way and this way, down to the river, away to the mountain; and all that tract is his. He walks to and fro. He says to himself: "It is a good land." He comes back home, and says to his wife, "Wife, we have got a grand inheritance."

That is the first thing he does.

The second is this. He gets some hurdles, and stakes off a part, and cultivates it. Next year he pushes the hurdles back, and takes more and cultivates that, and year after year he pushes the hurdles further back, until at last in twenty years his hurdles have reached the extent of his territory, and he has brought the whole of it under cultivation.

Now come with me. Come climb this mountain, the mountain of the Holy Ghost's teaching, and (1) *see what a Christ we have got;* and before I close we will encircle a little bit of Christ, we will (2) *take Him.* To-morrow we will push the hurdle further out, and take more of Christ, and the day after more, and the week after more, and year after year more. Only in eternity you will never put your fence of occupation on the margin of Christ's fullness, for when you have gone your furthest, still Christ will be eternally more.

Now see what Christ is. Look at I Corinthians 2:12: "That we might know the things that are freely given to us of God."

They tell me that George Macdonald, wanting to teach his children honor and truth and trust, places on the mantelshelf of the common room in their house, money enough for the whole use of his family. If the wife wants money she goes for it, if the boys and girls want money they go for it; whatever want there is in that house is supplied from that mantel-shelf deposit. So God put in Jesus everything the soul can want, and He says, "Go and take it. It is all there for you."

Are you in sorrow? In Christ there is joy. Are you tempted? In Christ there is succor. Are you at the end of your strength? In Jesus there is might. I recall those words, however, because you might think that God gives this or that apart from Christ. Let me put it more correctly so: you take Christ to be whatever you want, and He is the supply of your want, your need, so that you are blessed with all spiritual blessings in Christ in heavenly places. All that you want is in Christ, and I think it is a good thing to want in order to learn what there is in Christ.

I remember when I was a boy my mother never took so much notice of me as when I was disappointed and weak and ill and worn. I think sometimes I used to sham a bit because my mother always did so much for me then. It is when you are weak and weary, and your faith has gone, and your strength is exhausted, and your hopes are vanishing, and everything around is passing from your grasp—it is then that God comes and says, "Child, I have put into Jesus everything your spirit wants"; and though, like Madam Guyon, you have to spend ten years in jail, Christ will be friends and comfort and strength and society, and all you want.

Would that people might understand what Jesus can be to the soul—these people who have been going into society, to the play, to the opera, to worldly pleasure, into the old past, thinking that they must obtain peace and joy in them, and they are only disappointed! Would that I could tell them that in Jesus they have mountains and lakes and rivers and streams and treasures and cornfields and olive yards, and everything a soul can want to make it blessed! Spirit of God, take of the things of Christ and reveal them to every waiting heart!

I now want you to see

HOW TO TAKE

because John says that of His fullness we have all *received,* and Paul says that they which *receive* abundance of life shall reign. RECEIVE.

Do you know how to receive? You say, "Sir, I suppose you mean, I need to pray."

No sir, I do not mean that. You have been praying long enough. I want you to leave off praying in a sense, and to begin taking. There is all the difference in the world between praying for Christ and taking Christ. I will explain. Years ago, I was staying with Canon Wilberforce at Southampton—it was in the first flush of my new surrender. One autumn night he said, "We will sit around the fire and give our experiences."

Lord Radstock sat next to me, and he commenced. I followed, and talked as a young convert to this great teaching will talk—a good deal about my surrender to Christ. An old clergyman who sat on the other side of the circle, arose and said, "I am very startled that Mr. Meyer has nothing better than that. To hear him talk you would suppose that we had only got to give up. Now my religion is *taking in,* taking in first, and dropping and and giving up afterwards."

When you get gold you part with dross, and when you get real diamonds you part with paste. Get Christ, and the world attracts you no more. Give me sunlight, and I will dispense with electric light. Give me the light of day, I need no artificial luminary.

He continued, "I used once to be overcome by temper. I fought against temper. I came to the end of myself one afternoon when a number of children refused to listen to my teaching. I was on the point of losing my temper, when I turned to Christ, and said, 'Christ, be my sweet temper.'"

Instead of fighting against bad temper, he took Christ to be his patience, his humility, his meekness, his self-control. I saw in a moment that it was a better experience. I remember next morning when Canon Wilberforce came downstairs, as we stood together he said, "What did you think of that last night?"

I replied, "I think it will mark an era in my life."

He said, "It will do the same in mine."

From that moment I have tried to live that way, and whatever I have needed, I have said, "Christ, be this in me." That is the good fruit of the land.

Will you take this? Jesus does love you. Jesus is always near you. I do not talk about the cross so much as about Jesus who was crucified. I do not talk about the grave, but about Jesus who rose. I do not talk about the ascension, but about Jesus who ascended. He is with you and me always. It is not holiness, but it is Jesus the holy one. It is not meekness, it is Jesus the meek one. It is not purity, it is Jesus the pure one, Jesus, Jesus, Jesus! not *it*, not an *experience*, not *emotion*, not *faith*, but JESUS.

You have been worrying about your faith. Give it up! Do not think about your faith; think about Jesus, and you will have faith without knowing it. You have been worrying about your feeling. It does not matter, it goes up and down with the barometer. Have done with it, and live in the presence of Jesus.

Soul, thou and Jesus are standing face to face. Give thy whole self to Him and He gives His whole self to thee. Go to your bare garret, go to your dying child, go to scenes of trouble and sorrow and pain, He goes too. You have got the fountain beside you. You do not need to take your pitcher and go to draw in some external well. You have Jesus in your heart, a fountain springing up to everlasting life.

O soul, how rich thou art, who, passing through Jordan hast come into the good land of rest!

DELIVERANCE FROM THE POWER OF SIN

PHILIPPIANS 2:12, 13: "Work out your own salvation with fear and trembling. For it is God which worketh in you both to will and to do of His good pleasure."

Salvation. "Work out your own salvation." There is a sense in which salvation is finished. There is another sense in which it is in process. Finished by Christ when He died, and yet in process by the Holy Ghost in our heart.

Salvation is a great prize, with two termini. The first terminus is on the cross, where Jesus saved from the guilt, the penalty of sin; the second terminus is in His second Advent, when the body will be raised and married to the spirit, and salvation will be complete. But between His cross where Jesus put away guilt, and the second Advent where the body is married to the spirit, between these two there is the process of being saved from the power and the love of sin.

In Acts 2:47, and I Corinthians 1:18, the Revised Version in each case speaks of people being saved. "The Lord added to them day by day those that were being saved." "The word of the cross is to them that are perishing, foolishness: but unto us which are being saved it is the power of God."

A man says to me, "Are you saved?"

I reply, "I *was* saved when I trusted Christ; I *shall be* saved when my body is raised; but I am *being saved* all the time." Aye, we are being saved.

Remember that *sin is a parasite.* Your little babe has got measles, scarlatina, scarlet fever; but measles, scarlatina, scarlet fever are not native to it—they are parasites; and it is possible that in a few days they will pass, and your child's skin will be better. So sin is not necessary to human nature. Adam was created without it. Christ, a man, lived without it, and we men and women some day will have got over our mumps and measles and bronchitis, and we shall be whole.

Sin is a parasite. Thank God, the day will come when I shall stand up before my God without a stick or stone of sin. I may carry some scar that sin has left, but sin itself will be gone forever.

NEXT: *God comes into your heart to take your side against the parasite sin.*

A dear friend of mine told me that her boy came back from school with scarlet fever. He came home in a carriage, wrapped in blankets. As he was brought into the hall, she met him and said, "My boy, mother has got a room upstairs for you and herself, and mother is going to sit down by your bed, and she is never going to leave it till you are well, and mother is going to help you fight against the fever."

And she shut herself up in the bed-room with him. Do you think she loved the boy less because he was so long getting well? Once he said to her, "Mother, you have not kissed me lately. Don't you love me quite so much because I have got all these marks?"

She kissed him, and said, "I loved you before, but I think I love you better now."

So, dear soul, cursed with the sin which thou hast taken into thy heart, God hates the sin, but He loves thee! He knew all about it before He chose thee. He will never be surprised. He will never be disappointed. He will never love you less. But the more sinful you are, the weaker you are, the more often you have a relapse and go back, the more often you fall, the mother in God—for there is mother as well as father in God—the mother in God who has come into your heart will fight sin step by step with you. Your weakness will command His strongest love.

He sits down beside you. The fever is on your head and body. He knows it will take long vigil, long care, long patience. He has counted the cost, He is prepared for a long sickness. He has taken you in hand, your passions, your impurity, your garrulous gossip, your sulkiness, your jealousy, your vainglory, your love of money, your love of sin; God knows it all. But He has come, and will never leave you for a moment. If you will let Him, He will make short work. If you resist Him, you will make the work longer. But He will never leave you, He will never give you up, and however often you fall, go back to Him again.

Suppose some mother had a boy with scarlet fever, and in the fever he got delirious, and instead of keeping in bed he kept getting out; it would be very trying, very disappointing. He would throw his recovery back, but the mother would still cling to him. She would be sorry, and disappointed, and wish he had not done it; but she would love him, she could not give the boy up, she would bring him through.

O soul, thou hast thought ill of thy God! Thou hast thought because thou didst so often fall that God was tired of thee. Ah! thou knowest not that His tender mercy is infinite, and He will never let you go, NEVER, until in heaven He kisses your face, out of which the fever and the brand of sin have gone forever. O, my God, thou wilt kiss my soul into health!

Remember further that *His purpose is to deliver from the power of sin*. The *guilt* is gone, but the *power* remains, and He can only deliver from this gradually. Now, understand me. People ask if I believe in progressive or instantaneous sanctification. I reply—first, I do not believe in sanctification, I believe in the Sanctifier; I do not believe in holiness, I believe in the Holy One. Not an *it,* but *a person;* not an attribute, but Christ in my heart. *Instantaneous?* Yes, in this way: that in a moment I can take up the true attitude toward Christ: but *progressive,* because stage after stage He will carry on His work within me, weaning me, saving me from the love and the power of sin, deeper, deeper, deeper down into my heart. I take up the position suddenly, but I apply the position all along my life.

Is not this true? To-day you see things to be wrong which five years ago you permitted, and five years from to-day you will see things wrong which you now permit. Evidently the work is progressive. God sheds light upon our life. It is but the twilight at first. In the twilight I can see a chair and a table and a piano and a chiffonier: that is all. But the twilight merges into morning, and in the morning light I can see smaller things: the ornaments, the pictures that are on the wall. But morning becomes noon, and now I see the dust which has gathered. I could not see that in the twilight, but I see it at noon.

So God deals with you and me. He does not turn the heart upside down, and empty it of every sin at once. First the twilight, and we put away obvious sin; then morning, and we put away other sins not seen before; then eleven o'clock in the morning, and we put away deeper sins that we had missed; until it comes toward meridian, and in the perfect light we put away more sins, the small dust we had missed. We see deeper, deeper down, and every year a man is saved more completely from the power of known sin. So it is gradual.

I think it is perfectly absurd for a man to say he is perfectly sanctified. He is not within a thousand miles of it. Once, when in Leicester, I was paying parochial calls, and dropped in on a washerwoman who had just got out a line of clothes. I congratulated my friend because they looked so white. So, very much encouraged by her pastor's kind words, she asked him to have a cup of tea, and we sat down. While we were taking the tea, the sky clouded and there was a snow-storm; and as I came out the white snow lay everywhere, and I said to her, "Your washing does not look quite so clean as it did."

"Ah," she said, "the washing is white enough; but what can stand against God Almighty's white?"

So you may think that you are clean, because you have never seen God. When you see God, your holiest day will seem to be imperfect; you will abhor yourself and repent in dust and ashes, and you will need to say, "Forgive me my debts as I forgive my debtors."

SALVATION FROM KNOWN SIN—BUT NOT FROM TEMPTATION

Still, up to the limit of our light God can keep us from known sin. I will say that again: up to the limit of our light—twilight, morning, noon—up to the limit of our light God is able to keep us from all conscious and known sin. But He will not keep us from temptation. You cannot help the devil knocking at the door, but you can help inviting him in to supper. You cannot help the foul vulture flying over your head, but you can help letting him make a nest in your hair.

When you live near God you will be most tempted of the devil. Some men seem to think they are not holy because they are tempted. I should not believe in a man's holiness if he were not tempted. When I was at school, the boys used to avoid certain orchards, because they were full of crab apples; and you might know that the apples in those orchards were sour, or the boys would go for them. And if you are not tempted, it shows that your heart is empty and wicked, and

NOT WORTH THE DEVIL'S WHILE

to spend his time over. When the Spirit of God descended upon Christ He was led by the Spirit into the wilderness to be tempted of the devil—Spirit-filled, devil-tempted.

You ask, Why does God let us be tempted? I think it is to show where we are weak; that upon the temptation, as our stepping stone, we may reach out for some of God's help. I would not know how much I needed Christ unless the devil were constantly tempting me.

God is working in you. The compunction you feel when you sin, the yearning you feel for a better life, your